Maths Facts

Developing Problem Solving Skills in the Daily Maths Lesson

YEAR 1

Peter Clarke

Published by Collins Educational
An imprint of HarperCollins*Publishers* Ltd
77-85 Fulham Palace Road
Hammersmith
London
W6 8JB

www.**Collins**Education.com
On-line Support for Schools and Colleges

First published 2003

10 9 8 7 6 5 4 3 2 1

The author and publishers have done their best to ensure the accuracy of all the
information in *Maths Facts* Year 1.

Acknowledgement
A special thanks to Brian Molyneaux. Without his help, and persistence on the Internet,
this book would never have been written.

ISBN 0-00-715557-3

Publishing Manager: Melanie Hoffman
Project Editor: Ashley Lodge
Editor: Joan Miller
Cover design by Chi Leung
Cover illustration by Tony Wilkins
Series design by Neil Adams
Illustrations by Sascha Lipscomb, Juliet Breese, Roy Mitchell

Printed by Marlins the Printers, Berwick on Tweed

Contents

Contents

Introduction

Maths Facts is a series of six books for Year 1 to Year 6. It uses topics taught in Science, Geography and History lessons to practise and consolidate the problem solving strand of the National Numeracy Strategy (NNS) *Framework for teaching mathematics from Reception to Year 6*. At the same time it develops other key mathematical concepts and skills from the numbers and the number system, calculations and measures, shape and space strands of the Framework.

This book contains 40 activities for a Year 1 class. Each activity consists of two parts. The first presents facts which cover the units and topics suggested in the Science, Geography and History programmes of study in the National Curriculum, and the relevant Qualifications and Curriculum Authority (QCA) schemes of work. The second part presents mathematical word problems which the children will answer by referring back to the relevant information they have been given.

Maths Facts not only develops children's mathematical ability but also reinforces the topics learnt in Science, Geography and History lessons and provides familiar and relevant contexts for the children to apply their problem solving skills.

The questions for each activity are differentiated into three levels: A, B and C. This caters for the needs of different ability groups within the class and enables each *Maths Facts* activity to be used at any time throughout the year.

Mathematical problem solving

Mathematical problem solving includes *applying mathematics* to the solution of problems arising from the environment and *reasoning* about questions that have arisen from the mathematics itself. Being able to use mathematics to analyse situations and solve real-life problems is a major reason for studying the subject. Frequent use of everyday scenarios will give meaning to the children's mathematical experiences. Children need to be able to apply the mathematics they have learned to real-life situations in their environment. They also need to be able to interpret and make meaning from their results. Teachers need to structure situations in which children investigate problems that are relevant to their daily lives and that relate to the mathematical knowledge, skills and understanding the children have most recently acquired.

Children also need to be made aware of the mathematics they are using to solve problems. Encouraging them to think about and discuss the strategies they use, and the knowledge and skills they have acquired, will assist children in developing a deeper understanding of mathematics. Discussions that arise out of mathematical problem solving can help children share experiences with each other and gain new knowledge, and will also assist them in developing their own mathematical vocabulary.

Problem solving skills

Maths Facts aims to develop in children the key skills required to tackle and solve mathematical problems. These include:

- reading and making sense of a problem

- recognising key words, relevant information and redundant information

- finding parts of a problem that can be tackled

- recognising the mathematics that can be used to help solve a problem

- deciding which number operation(s) to perform and in which order

- choosing an efficient way of calculating

- changing measurements to the same units before calculating

- getting into the habit of checking their own work to see whether the answer makes sense.

Strategies for solving mathematical problems

If children are to solve mathematical problems successfully they must be taught not only the mathematical concepts but also the strategies and procedures needed to apply these concepts. Children need to be taught to:

- look for a pattern or sequence
- experiment or act out a problem
- make a drawing or model
- make a list, table or chart
- write a number sentence
- see mathematical connections

- make and test a prediction
- make a generalisation
- establish a proof
- account for all known possibilities
- solve a simpler related problem
- work backwards.

An approach to solving mathematical problems

Children need to develop an effective and efficient method for solving mathematical problems. Page 7 provides them with a step-by-step approach to solving mathematical word problems. Photocopy and enlarge this page into a poster, and display it for all the class to see and follow during problem solving activities.

The seven steps to problem solving

Step 1   Read the problem.

Step 2   What do you have to find?

Step 3   What facts are given?

Step 4   Which facts do you need?

Step 5   Make a plan.

Step 6   Carry out your plan to find an answer.

Step 7   Check your answer.

Common pupil difficulties in problem solving

Sometimes children who are confident and capable at solving purely mathematical exercises, such as calculations, experience difficulties when it comes to solving problems. This may be due to difficulties with one or more of the following:

- reading the problem with understanding
- selecting the relevant information
- using the necessary mathematical expression
- making the required calculation correctly
- seeing relationships and using patterns
- using existing mathematical knowledge
- developing a systematic approach
- estimating the answer
- using trial-and-improvement techniques
- checking the answer
- seeing if the answer is reasonable
- recognising the connection between the answer achieved and the question asked
- being motivated
- perseverance
- confidence.

Suggestions for overcoming common pupil difficulties in problem solving

One or more of these strategies may help children who are experiencing difficulties with solving a problem.

- Present the problem orally.
- Discuss a possible approach with the children, asking appropriate questions.
- Revise any mathematical knowledge or skills needed to solve the problem successfully.
- Allow the children to work together, sharing their ideas for tackling a problem.
- Use smaller numbers.
- Use a pictorial approach if children are having difficulty with the abstract form of the problem.
- Use concrete apparatus to clarify the mathematics for the children.

- Allow the children to use appropriate resources such as a number line or hundred square to assist them with the mathematics.
- Allow the children to use a calculator.
- Use problems that are of relevance and interest to the children.

The teacher's role in problem solving lessons

- Give a choice where possible.
- Present the problem verbally, giving maximum visual support where appropriate.
- Enable children to own the problem.
- Encourage children to work together, sharing ideas for tackling a problem.
- Allow time and space for collaboration and consultation.
- Intervene, when asked, in such a way as to develop children's autonomy and independence.
- Encourage children to report the progress they are making.
- Work alongside children, setting an example yourself.
- Encourage the children to present their work to others.

The four types of word problem

All the activities in this book provide a balance between the four different types of word problem.

- The final quantity is unknown, e.g.

  – *Samantha has £1.35 and Jeanette has £1.65. How much money do they have altogether?*

  – *Matz baked 12 small cakes in each cake tin. He used two full tins. How many cakes did he bake?*

  – *Michael shared 20 grapes equally among himself and his four friends. How many did each person get?*

- The final quantity is known but not all the steps on the way, e.g.

  – *Berinda's mum baked 20 cookies. Berinda's friends came to play and ate some. How many were eaten if there were only 12 cookies left?*

  – *Sylvia needs 14 eggs. Each carton holds 6 eggs. How many cartons does she need?*

  – *Sam had 15 plants in a flowerbed. He decided to throw out all the plants that were dying. He threw out 8 plants. How many plants did he keep?*

- Multi-step problems, e.g.

  - *There are 12 people on a bus. At the next stop 8 people get on and 5 get off. How many people are there on the bus now?*

  - *Steven's parents are taking Steven and his 2 sisters to the fun fair. Tickets cost £15.00 for adults and £12.50 for children. How much change do Steven's parents receive from £100?*

  - *I have enough wheels for 3 cars and there will be 2 over. How many wheels do I have?*

- Problems that involve comparisons between two or more sets, e.g.

  - *The number 59 bus has 16 people sitting downstairs and 27 people sitting upstairs. How many more people are sitting upstairs than are sitting downstairs?*

  - *I have 5 marbles, Louis has 3 and Brian has 12. Who has most? How many more does Brian have than Louis? How many more does Brian have than I do? How many more do I have than Louis?*

Maths Facts and the teaching–learning cycle

Assessment

- Guidance given on how to record pupil performance in AT1 – *Using and applying mathematics*.

Teaching

- Consistent and easy-to-follow format for each activity.
- Guidance given on how to incorporate *Maths Facts* into the daily mathematics lesson.

Planning

- All activities provide practice and consolidation of the problem solving objectives in the NNS *Framework for teaching mathematics from Reception to Year 6*.
- Reference given to other relevant National Curriculum subjects, including National Curriculum programmes of study and QCA Primary schemes of work.
- Guidance given for planning a programme of work.

Maths Facts and the daily mathematics lesson

The activities contained in *Maths Facts* are ideally suited to the daily mathematics lesson. Each activity is designed to be introduced to the whole class or group. A suggestion for a possible structure to a lesson using *Maths Facts* is given below.

- Oral work and mental calculation

  - Warm up the class by consolidating the knowledge and skills that will be used to solve the word problems.

  - Stimulate their involvement.

  - Emphasise the key vocabulary.

- Main teaching activity

  - Introduce the activity sheet to the children. Ensure that the children understand the picture and/or the vocabulary on the sheet.

  - Work through a couple of questions with the whole class, stressing possible problem solving strategies used.

  - Ask children to work in pairs on one or two of the problems.

  - Discuss these problems as a whole class.

- Pupil consolidation activities

  - Direct children's attention to the differentiated level(s) most appropriate to their needs.

  - Allow children to work individually or in pairs to solve the word problems.

  - Where needed, provide appropriate resources to assist children with the mathematics.

  - Monitor individuals, pairs or groups of children, offering support when and where necessary.

- Plenary

  - Plan an extended plenary.

  - Discuss one or two problems and possible solutions and strategies in depth with the whole class.

  - Give answers only to the remaining problems.

Curriculum information

The activities in this book provide children with an opportunity to practise and consolidate the following Year 1 problem solving objectives.

- Topic: *Making decisions*

  - Choose and use appropriate number operations and mental strategies to solve problems.

- Topic: *Reasoning about numbers or shapes*

  - Solve simple mathematical problems or puzzles; recognise and predict from simple patterns and relationships. Suggest extensions by asking 'What if…?' or 'What could I try next?'

  - Investigate a general statement about familiar numbers or shapes by finding examples that satisfy it.

  - Explain methods and reasoning orally.

- Topic: *Problems involving 'real life', money or measures*

  - Use mental strategies to solve simple word problems set in 'real life', money or measurement contexts, using counting, addition, subtraction, doubling and halving, explaining methods and reasoning orally.

  - Recognise all coins of different values. Find totals and change up to 20p. Work out how to pay an exact sum using smaller coins.

- Topic: *Organising and using data*

  - Solve a given problem by sorting, classifying and organising information in simple ways, such as: using objects or pictures, in a list or simple table. Discuss and explain results.

The National Numeracy Strategy curriculum coverage chart on page 13 shows which activity is matched to which NNS strand and topic.

The chart on page 14 shows the theme for each *Maths Facts* activity and its link with the relevant National Curriculum programmes of study and QCA Primary schemes of work for Science, Geography and History.

National Numeracy Strategy curriculum coverage

Strand	Numbers and the number system			Calculations			Solving problems				Measures, shape and space	
Topic / Activity	Counting, properties of numbers and number sequences	Place value and ordering	Estimating	Understanding addition and subtraction	Rapid recall of addition and subtraction facts	Mental calculation Strategies (+ and −)	Making decisions	Reasoning about numbers or shapes	Problems involving: 'real life' (RL) money (MO) measures (ME)	Organising and using data	Measures: Length (L) Mass (M) Capacity (C) Time (T)	Shape and space
1				✔	✔	✔	✔	✔	RL			
2				✔	✔	✔	✔	✔	RL			
3	✔	✔		✔	✔	✔	✔	✔	RL			
4	✔			✔	✔	✔	✔	✔	RL			
5	✔			✔	✔	✔	✔	✔	RL			
6	✔			✔	✔	✔	✔	✔	RL			✔
7	✔			✔	✔	✔	✔	✔	RL			
8	✔			✔	✔	✔	✔	✔	RL			
9				✔	✔	✔	✔	✔	MO			
10				✔	✔	✔	✔	✔	MO			
11	✔	✔		✔	✔	✔	✔	✔	MO			
12	✔			✔	✔	✔	✔	✔	MO			
13		✔		✔	✔	✔	✔	✔	MO			
14	✔	✔	✔	✔	✔	✔	✔	✔	MO			
15	✔			✔	✔	✔	✔	✔	MO			
16		✔		✔	✔	✔	✔	✔	MO			
17	✔	✔		✔	✔	✔	✔	✔	ME		L	
18	✔			✔	✔	✔	✔	✔	ME		L	
19		✔		✔	✔	✔	✔	✔	ME		L	
20			✔	✔	✔	✔	✔	✔	ME		L	✔
21				✔	✔	✔	✔	✔	ME		T	
22				✔	✔	✔	✔	✔	ME		L/M/C/T	
23	✔			✔	✔	✔	✔	✔	ME		L/T	
24	✔			✔	✔	✔	✔	✔	ME		M/C/T	✔
25				✔	✔	✔	✔	✔	RL/ME		L/C/T	
26	✔			✔	✔	✔	✔	✔	RL/MO/ME		L/T	
27	✔			✔	✔	✔	✔	✔	RL/MO/ME		T	
28	✔			✔	✔	✔	✔	✔	RL/ME		L/T	✔
29	✔	✔		✔	✔	✔	✔	✔	RL/MO/ME		T	
30	✔			✔	✔	✔	✔	✔	RL/MO/ME		W/T	
31	✔			✔	✔	✔	✔	✔	RL/MO/ME		T	
32	✔	✔		✔	✔	✔	✔	✔	RL/MO/ME		L/T	
33	✔							✔		✔		
34	✔			✔	✔	✔	✔	✔		✔		
35	✔			✔	✔	✔	✔	✔		✔		
36	✔	✔						✔		✔		
37	✔			✔	✔	✔	✔	✔		✔		
38	✔	✔		✔	✔	✔	✔	✔		✔		
39	✔			✔	✔	✔	✔	✔		✔		
40	✔							✔		✔		

Links with National Curriculum programmes of study and QCA Primary schemes of work

Curriculum subject	Key Stage 1 National Curriculum programme of study	QCA Primary scheme of work	*Maths Facts* theme	Activity
Science	Sc2 Life processes and living things 1 Life processes 2 Humans and other animals 4 Variation and classification Breadth of study: 1/2	1A Ourselves	Our bodies	1
			Young and old	2
			Food and drink	9
			Measuring heights	17
			Humans and animals	33
			How are our bodies different?	34
	Sc2 Life processes and living things 1 Life processes 3 Green plants Breadth of study: 1/2	1B Growing plants	Food we eat from seeds	10
			Plants that feed us	18
			Growing a sunflower	35
	Sc3 Materials and their properties 1 Grouping materials Breadth of study: 1/2	1C Sorting and using materials	The hardware shop	11
			Making a cake	25
	Sc4 Physical processes 3 Light and sound Breadth of study: 1/2	1D Light and dark	Different lights	3
			Playing safe in the sun	4
			Fireworks	26
	Sc4 Physical processes 2 Forces and motion Breadth of study: 1/2	1E Pushes and pulls	The wind	5
			Skateboarders down a ramp	19
	Sc2 Life processes and living things 2 Humans and other animals Sc4 Physical processes 3 Light and sound Breadth of study: 1/2	1F Sound and hearing	Musical instruments	27
			Can Billy hear it?	36
Geography	Knowledge, skills and understanding 3 Knowledge and understanding of places 4 Knowledge and understanding of patterns and processes Breadth of study: 6	1 Around our school – the local area 24 Passport to the world 25 Geography and numbers	The post office	12
			The community sports centre	13
			Anita walks to school	20
			A map of Berry School	28
			Around Berry School	37
			How children in 1C come to school	38
	Knowledge, skills and understanding 3 Knowledge and understanding of places 5 Knowledge and understanding of environmental change and sustainable development Breadth of study: 6	2 How can we make our local area safer? 24 Passport to the world 25 Geography and numbers	Parking in Busy Street	21
			Safe Street and Busy Street	29
			Traffic in Safe Street and Busy Street	39
	Knowledge, skills and understanding 3 Knowledge and understanding of places Breadth of study: 6	5 Where in the world is Barnaby Bear? 24 Passport to the world 25 Geography and numbers	Barnaby's shopping list	14
			Barnaby's day in Paris	22
			Barnaby at the airport	30

Curriculum subject	Key Stage 1 National Curriculum programme of study	QCA Primary scheme of work	*Maths Facts* theme	Activity
History	Knowledge, skills and understanding 1 Chronological understanding 2 Knowledge and understanding of events, people and changes in the past Breadth of study: 6	1 How are our toys different from those in the past?	Old toys for sale	15
			The toy museum	31
			Sorting toys	40
	Knowledge, skills and understanding 1 Chronological understanding 2 Knowledge and understanding of events, people and changes in the past Breadth of study: 6	2 What were homes like a long time ago?	An Edwardian country house	6
			An Edwardian kitchen	7
			A Victorian sitting room	23
			A Victorian kitchen	24
	Knowledge, skills and understanding 1 Chronological understanding 2 Knowledge and understanding of events, people and changes in the past Breadth of study: 6	3 What were seaside holidays like in the past?	On the beach in 1900	8
			Annie's seaside holiday	16
			Beth's family photos	32

General guidance for Levels A, B and C in *Maths Facts* Year 1

Level A

Children should have been introduced to the following objectives:

- Count reliably at least 20 objects.

- Read and write numerals from 0 to at least 20.

- Order numbers to at least 20.

- Describe and extend number sequences: count on and back in ones from any small number, and in tens from and back to zero.

- Know by heart:
  - all pairs of numbers with a total of 10;
  - addition facts for all pairs of numbers with a total up to at least 5;
  - and the corresponding subtraction facts.

- Put the larger number first and count on in ones.

If children experience difficulty with questions at this level provide them with:

- a set of counting apparatus such as counters, buttons, interlocking cubes

- 0–10 number line

Level B

Children should have been introduced to the following objectives:

Level A objectives and:

- Begin to recognise that more than two numbers can be added together.

- Know by heart addition doubles for all numbers to at least 5.

- Begin to know by heart:
  - addition facts for all pairs of numbers with a total up to at least 10;
  - and the corresponding subtraction facts.
- Use known number facts and place value to add or subtract a pair of numbers mentally within the range 0 to at least 10, then 0 to at least 20.

If children experience difficulty with questions at this level provide them with:

- 0–20 number line

Level C

Children should have been introduced to the following objectives:

Level A and B objectives and:

- Begin to bridge through 10, and later 20, when adding a single-digit number.

If children experience difficulty with questions at this level provide them with:

- 0–20 number line

Planning a programme of work for *Maths Facts*

The *Maths Facts* Programme chart on page 17 may be used in conjunction with your long- and medium-term plans to develop a *Maths Facts* programme of work throughout the year. By following the topics allocated using the NNS *Framework for teaching mathematics from Reception to Year 6* or similar scheme of work, you will ensure that the children not only have an opportunity to practise and consolidate the topic and specific objectives for a particular week but also, where appropriate, link this with other National Curriculum subjects.

Maths Facts and assessment

Maths Facts activities may be used with the whole class or with groups of children as an assessment activity. Linked to the topic that is being studied at present, *Maths Facts* will provide you with an indication of how well the children have understood the objectives being covered as well as their problem solving skills.

The assessment and record-keeping format on page 18 can be used to assess and assign levels to individual children in Attainment Target 1: *Using and applying mathematics*. By observing individual children while they undertake a *Maths Facts* activity, discussing their work with them and subsequently marking their work, you will be able to gain a good understanding of their problem solving, communicating and reasoning skills. Your judgements about an individual child's abilities can then be entered onto the assessment and record-keeping format and this will provide you with an Attainment Target 1 level. It is envisaged that one copy of the assessment and record-keeping format would be used for your entire class.

Maths Facts Programme

Year: _____   Class: _____

Teacher: _____

	Week	Mathematics topic	Other National Curriculum subject and topic	*Maths Facts* activity
AUTUMN	1			
	2			
	3			
	4			
	5			
	6			
	7			
	8			
	9			
	10			
	11			
	12			
SPRING	1			
	2			
	3			
	4			
	5			
	6			
	7			
	8			
	9			
	10			
	11			
	12			
SUMMER	1			
	2			
	3			
	4			
	5			
	6			
	7			
	8			
	9			
	10			
	11			
	12			

Attainment Target 1: *Using and applying mathematics*
Assessment and record-keeping format

Year: _____ Class: _____

Teacher: _____

LEVEL 1

Problem solving
- Use mathematics as an integral part of classroom activities
- Use materials for a practical task

Communicating
- Represent work with objects or pictures and discuss it

Reasoning
- Recognise and use simple patterns or relationships

LEVEL 2

Problem solving
- Select and use material in some classroom activities
- Select and use mathematics for some classroom activities
- Begin to develop own strategies for solving a problem
- Begin to understand ways of working through a problem

Communicating
- Discuss work using mathematical language
- Respond to and ask mathematical questions
- Begin to represent work using symbols and simple diagrams
- Explain why an answer is correct

Reasoning
- Ask questions such as: 'What would happen if...?' 'Why?'
- Begin to develop simple strategies

LEVEL 3

Problem solving
- Develop different mathematical approaches to a problem
- Begin to explain thinking
- Look for ways to overcome difficulties
- Begin to make decisions and realise that results may vary according to the 'rule' used
- Begin to organise work
- Check results

Communicating
- Discuss mathematical work
- Begin to explain thinking
- Use and interpret mathematical symbols and diagrams

Reasoning
- Understand a general statement
- Investigate general statements and predictions by finding and trying out examples

GENERAL COMMENTS

Our bodies

Susie

Leo

> Show any working on the back of this sheet.

A 1 How many fingers do Leo and Susie have altogether?

2 There are 10 children in the pool. If 4 of them are girls, how many are boys?

3 Leo is 7 years old. How old will he be in 3 years' time?

B 1 Leo is 7 years old and Susie is 4 years old. What is the difference in their ages?

2 Leo and Susie each took two friends to the pool. How many friends did they take altogether?

3 How many fingers and toes do Leo and Susie have altogether?

C 1 Susie wears size 4 sandals and Leo wears size 8 sandals. How many sizes smaller are Susie's sandals than Leo's?

2 Leo can swim across the pool 12 times. Susie can swim across the pool 7 times less than Leo. How many times can Susie swim across the pool?

3 Leo had 20 baby teeth. Now 4 of them have fallen out. How many baby teeth does he have left?

Young and old

Mum   Dad   Sam   Alex

Josie   Kitty   Fido

Show any working on the back of this sheet.

A 1 Fido is 2 years old. How old will he be on his next birthday?

2 Kitty is 5 years old and Fido is 2 years old. How much older is Kitty than Fido?

3 Kitty is 5 years old. Sam is 2 years older than Kitty. How old is Sam?

B 1 Alex is 10 years old and Kitty is 5 years old. How old was Alex when Kitty was born?

2 Alex is 10 years old and Josie is 13 years old. What is the difference in their ages?

3 Josie is 13 years old and Fido is 2 years old. How old was Josie when Fido was born?

C 1 Alex is 10 years old. Dad was 30 years old when Alex was born. How old is Dad now?

2 Alex is 10 years old. Mum was 26 years old when Alex was born. How old is Mum now?

3 When Alex was born, Dad was 30 years old and Mum was 26 years old. How much older is Dad than Mum?

Problems involving 'real life'
Science: 1D. Light and dark

Name _____

Date _____

Different lights

Happy Birthday Steven

Show any working on the back of this sheet.

A 1 How many torches and lamps are there altogether?

2 There are fewer torches than Christmas lanterns. How many fewer?

3 How many more candles are there than torches?

B 1 If it was Steven's 10th birthday how many more candles should there be on the cake?

2 How many torches, candles and lamps are there altogether?

3 It is Steven's 8th birthday. In one breath he blew out 5 candles. How many candles were still alight on the cake?

C 1 How many more Hallowe'en lights are there than Christmas lanterns?

2 Dad changed half the bulbs in the Christmas lanterns because they were broken. How many bulbs did he change?

3 Mum bought another set of Hallowe'en lights. How many Hallowe'en lights did she have altogether?

Name _____

Date _____

Playing safe in the sun

Show any working on the back of this sheet.

Ⓐ 1 How many people are wearing a hat?

2 How many people altogether are in the picture?

3 How many people in the picture are wearing sunglasses and a hat?

Ⓑ 1 How many more children are on the sand than on a beach mat?

2 There are more people wearing a hat than not wearing a hat. How many more?

3 5 more people put on sunglasses. How many people are now wearing sunglasses?

Ⓒ 1 4 people take off their hats. How many people are now wearing hats?

2 If 7 more people go into the sea, how many people are left on the beach?

3 7 people were in the sea. Another 5 people go into the sea. How many people altogether are in the sea now?

The wind

Show any working
on the back of
this sheet.

A **1** How many socks are on the washing line? ☐

2 What is the total number of seagulls and sailing boats? ☐

3 3 more pairs of shorts are put on the washing line.
How many pairs of shorts are on the line altogether? ☐

B **1** How many boats and clouds are there altogether? ☐

2 How many more clouds than birds are there? ☐

3 The wind blows away 1 shirt and 1 tea towel. How many
shirts and tea towels are left on the line? ☐

C **1** This morning there were 5 fewer clouds in the sky than
there are now. How many clouds were there this morning? ☐

2 5 sailing boats have already sailed by. How many sailing
boats is that altogether? ☐

3 There are 6 more socks to go on the line. How many
socks will this be altogether? ☐

Activity 6

Problems involving 'real life'
History: 2. What were homes like
a long time ago?

Name _____

Date _____

An Edwardian country house

> Show any working on
> the back of this sheet.

A 1 How many windows does the house have altogether?

2 How many windows are there on the ground floor?

3 The maid has cleaned 3 steps. There are 3 more steps
to clean. How many steps are there altogether?

B 1 How many more windows are there on the ground floor
than on the top floor?

2 10 ladies and 10 men are having dinner tonight. How many
people will be having dinner altogether?

3 2 cooks and 7 maids prepare dinner. How many people
prepare dinner?

C 1 The house has 6 rooms on the ground floor and 8 rooms on
the first floor. How many rooms is this altogether?

2 Billy is cleaning the windows on the first floor. He has
already cleaned 6 of the windows. How many more windows
does he have to clean?

3 4 windows are square and 21 windows are in the shape of
a rectangle. How many more windows are in the shape of a
rectangle than a square?

Activity 7

Problems involving 'real life'
History: 2. What were homes like a long time ago?

Name _____

Date _____

An Edwardian kitchen

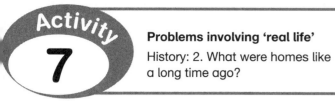

Show any working on the back of this sheet.

A **1** How many jugs and cups are there altogether?

2 How many pans are there altogether?

3 There were 10 cups but some of them got broken. How many cups were broken?

B **1** The cook has taken 3 cookbooks from the shelf. How many cookbooks are there altogether?

2 The cook needs to use 3 pans to cook lunch. How many pans will she not be using?

3 Half the small plates will be used for lunch. How many will be used?

C **1** In one of the drawers there are 10 knives, 10 forks and 10 spoons. How many knives, forks and spoons are there altogether?

2 There are the same number of large plates as small plates. Some of the large plates are being used. How many large plates are being used?

3 There are 12 cakes baking in the oven. If 3 of them get burnt, how many cakes will be left?

Activity 8

Problems involving 'real life'
History: 3. What were seaside
holidays like in the past?

Name _____

Date _____

On the beach in 1900

Show any working on
the back of this sheet.

A 1 How many people are wearing hats or caps?

2 How many people are not in the sea?

3 If 2 of the children go for a donkey ride, how many people
altogether will be riding donkeys?

B 1 There are 6 children in the family. How many more girls
than boys are there in the family?

2 There are 6 bathing huts. People are using 4 of them.
How many bathing huts are not being used?

3 Each donkey can carry 2 people. If 8 people go for a donkey
ride, how many donkeys are needed?

C 1 The people in the sea have left their shoes in the bathing huts.
How many shoes are in the bathing huts?

2 The people in the sea and one lady go home. How many
people are still on the beach?

3 There are 4 donkeys. How many donkey legs are there
altogether?

Food and drink

Gates Primary School
SPORTS DAY

Prices
Bag of crisps...12p
Cheese stick......8p
Apple..................5p
Orange...............6p
Cup of orange
squash..............10p

Show any working on
the back of this sheet.

A 1 How many things cost less than 7p?

2 Lee buys a cheese stick. What change from 10p will she get?

3 Tim buys an orange. What is his change from 10p?

B 1 What is the difference in price between a cheese stick and
an apple?

2 Gita buys a cheese stick. She uses 3 coins to pay
the exact price. Which 3 coins does she use?

3 Sanjay buys an orange and pays with a 20p coin.
What is his change?

C 1 Sam buys a bag of crisps and a cup of orange squash.
How much does he spend?

2 Ami buys an apple and a cup of orange squash. How much
change will she get from 20p?

3 Ahmed buys an apple and a cheese stick for himself, and
a bag of crisps for his sister. How much does he spend?

Food we eat from seeds

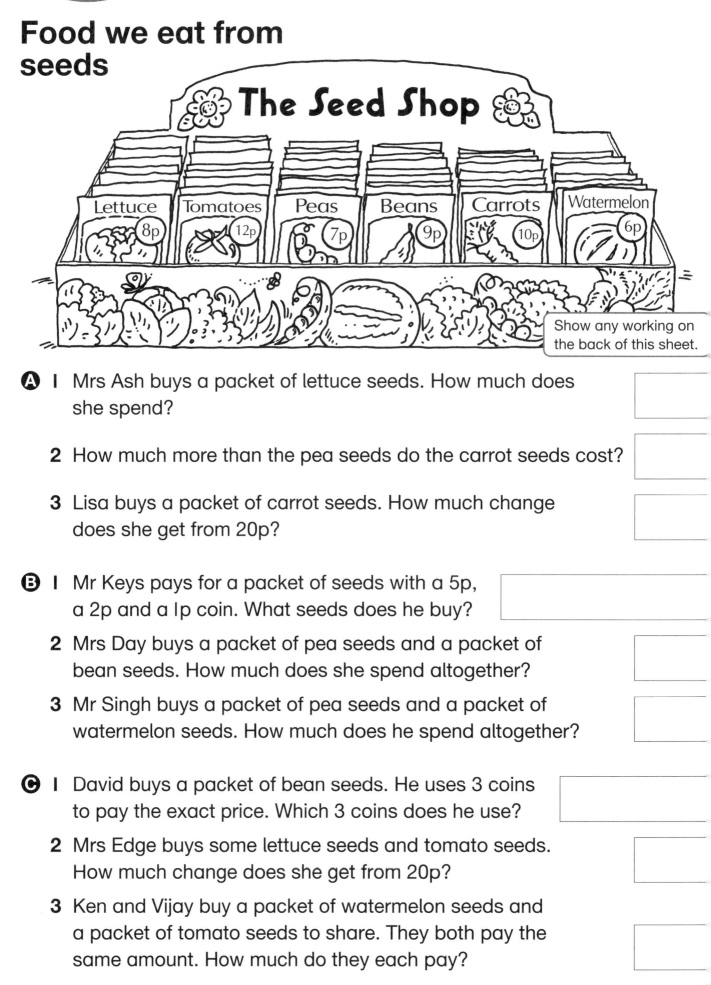

The Seed Shop

Lettuce 8p | Tomatoes 12p | Peas 7p | Beans 9p | Carrots 10p | Watermelon 6p

Show any working on the back of this sheet.

A 1 Mrs Ash buys a packet of lettuce seeds. How much does she spend?

2 How much more than the pea seeds do the carrot seeds cost?

3 Lisa buys a packet of carrot seeds. How much change does she get from 20p?

B 1 Mr Keys pays for a packet of seeds with a 5p, a 2p and a 1p coin. What seeds does he buy?

2 Mrs Day buys a packet of pea seeds and a packet of bean seeds. How much does she spend altogether?

3 Mr Singh buys a packet of pea seeds and a packet of watermelon seeds. How much does he spend altogether?

C 1 David buys a packet of bean seeds. He uses 3 coins to pay the exact price. Which 3 coins does he use?

2 Mrs Edge buys some lettuce seeds and tomato seeds. How much change does she get from 20p?

3 Ken and Vijay buy a packet of watermelon seeds and a packet of tomato seeds to share. They both pay the same amount. How much do they each pay?

The hardware shop

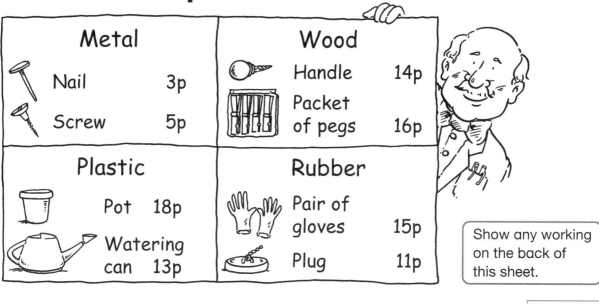

Show any working on the back of this sheet.

A 1 How many different things are shown on the poster?

   2 How much cheaper is a nail than a screw?

   3 Put the prices in order, starting with the lowest.

B 1 Sonny uses two 5p coins and a 1p coin to pay the exact price for something. What does he buy?

   2 Jamie buys a pot. How much change does he get from 20p?

   3 Steve buys 2 screws and 2 nails. How much will they cost?

C 1 Lisa buys a packet of pegs. She uses 3 coins to pay the exact price. Which 3 coins does she use?

   2 What is the difference between the prices of the pot and the plug?

   3 Simon bought one thing in the shop. He gave the shopkeeper a 10p coin and a 5p coin. The shopkeeper gave him 2p change. What did Simon buy?

Activity
12

Problems involving money
Geography: 1. Around our
school – the local area

Name _____

Date _____

The post office

Stamps

........1p

........2p

........4p

........5p

......10p

......12p

Show any working on
the back of this sheet.

A 1 How many different types of stamp are for sale?

  2 David buys a 1p stamp and a 2p stamp. How much is
that altogether?

  3 Mrs Monks buys a 2p stamp and a 4p stamp. How much
does she spend altogether?

B 1 Larry buys two 10p stamps. How much is that altogether?

  2 If Ben buys a 12p stamp, how much change does he get
from 20p?

  3 Jan buys a 2p stamp, a 4p stamp and a 10p stamp.
How much is that altogether?

C 1 Mrs James buys a 10p stamp and a 5p stamp. How much
change does she get from 20p?

  2 The lady in the post office has just sold five 10p stamps.
How much is that altogether?

  3 Mr Brown wants to post a letter. It will cost him 22p.
Which two stamps does he buy?

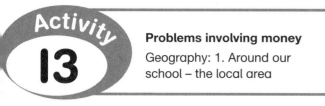

Activity 13

Problems involving money
Geography: 1. Around our
school – the local area

Name _____

Date _____

The community sports centre

Community Sports Centre Open Day

**Come to your local sports centre and enjoy
all the activities for less than 20p each**

Tennis	6p each	Bowling	16p each
Swimming	5p each	Roller skating	12p each
Bicycling	14p each	Squash	9p each

Show any working on
the back of this sheet.

Ⓐ 1 Which sport costs the most?

2 How much more does it cost to play tennis than to go
swimming?

3 Write the prices of the 6 sports in order, starting
with the smallest.

Ⓑ 1 2 friends play tennis. How much does it cost them altogether?

2 Ali goes swimming and then bicycling. How much does it
cost him altogether?

3 How much more does it cost to go roller skating than to
play tennis?

Ⓒ 1 Susan has 20p. Does she have enough money to go
swimming and bowling?

2 Allison did just one thing at the sports centre. She paid
for it with a 5p coin and two 2p coins.
What did she do at the sports centre?

3 In the morning Matt played tennis and then went swimming.
In the afternoon he played squash. How much did Matt
spend altogether at the sports centre?

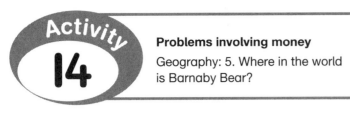

Activity 14

Problems involving money
Geography: 5. Where in the world is Barnaby Bear?

Name _____

Date _____

Barnaby's shopping list

Show any working on the back of this sheet.

A 1 How many things does Barnaby have on his list?

2 How many things on his list cost more than 8p?

3 Put in order the prices that Barnaby pays, starting with the lowest.

B 1 Barnaby goes to the sweet shop. He buys his bag of sweets and bottle of squash. How much does he spend?

2 Barnaby goes to the chemist and buys the comb and the toothbrush. How much does he spend?

3 Barnaby buys the pencil and paper in the same shop. How much change does he get from 15p?

C 1 The comb costs less than the toothbrush. How much less?

2 Barnaby buys the needle, the thread and the handkerchief in one shop. He pays with one coin and gets no change. What coin does he use?

3 Roughly how much does Barnaby spend altogether – 30p, 50p or 80p?

Maths Facts (Y1) © HarperCollins*Publishers* Ltd 2003

Activity
15

Problems involving money
History: 1. How are our toys
different from those in the past?

Name _____

Date _____

Old toys for sale

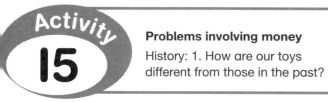

train 16p

doll 6p

car 12p

toy soldier 8p

marbles 4p

spinning top 9p

skipping rope 7p

merry-go-round 17p

blocks 10p

yo-yo 5p

horse 13p

skittles 10p

Bring & Buy Sale

Show any working on the back of this sheet.

A 1 How many different toys are for sale?

2 Which 2 toys cost the same?

3 Sunita buys the doll. How much change does she get from 10p?

B 1 At the end of the day 9 toys have been sold. How many toys are left?

2 Jerry buys the blocks and the car. How much does it cost him altogether?

3 Henry has two 20p coins. Does he have enough money to buy the merry-go-round and the train?

C 1 Simone buys the horse. She uses 3 coins to pay the exact price. Which 3 coins did she use?

2 The merry-go-round costs more than the toy soldier. How much more?

3 Declan buys the yo-yo, the marbles and the spinning top. How much does he spend altogether?

Activity 16

Problems involving money
History: 3. What were seaside
holidays like in the past?

Name _____

Date _____

Annie's seaside holiday

Show any working on
the back of this sheet.

A 1 Annie went to the Punch and Judy show. She paid with
a 5p coin. What change did she get?

2 Mum and Dad each hired a deck chair. How much did
they pay altogether?

3 Put the ticket prices in order, starting with the smallest.

B 1 Annie went for a steam train ride. She paid for the ride with
one coin and got 1p change. Which coin did she pay with?

2 Annie's parents gave her 20p to spend. Did she have enough
money to go on the big dipper and have a donkey ride?

3 Annie, Tom, Mum and Dad went for a walk along the pier.
How much did it cost them altogether?

C 1 Tom went for a donkey ride. He used 3 coins to
pay the exact price. Which 3 coins did he use?

2 Mum and Dad both went for a donkey ride. How much did
it cost them altogether?

3 Annie had a donkey ride and Tom took a train ride.
How much did they pay altogether?

Measuring heights

Mrs James

Jini

Ali   Sam   Gita   Leo

Show any working
on the back of
this sheet.

A 1 How many people are there in the picture?

2 Baby Leo is 4 blocks tall. How many blocks tall
is Ali?

3 Write the names of the people in order, shortest to tallest.

B 1 Gita is 10 blocks tall. Baby Leo is 4 blocks tall.
How much taller is Gita than Leo?

2 Gita is 10 blocks tall. Her balloon is 5 blocks higher
than she is. How high is her balloon?

3 Jini is 13 blocks tall. Her doll is 3 blocks tall. Jini
stands her doll on top of her head. How tall are
Jini and her doll altogether?

C 1 Sam is 15 blocks tall. His cricket bat is 6 blocks
long. How much taller is Sam than his cricket bat?

2 Mrs James is 16 blocks tall. Jini is 13 blocks tall.
How much taller is Mrs James than Jini?

3 Sam is 15 blocks tall and Jini is 13 blocks tall.
Sam and Jini lie in a line, head to toe. How long
are they altogether?

Plants that feed us

Farmer Fred measured the heights of the fruit and vegetables that he grew.

16   12   8   7   5   3   1

apple tree   sunflower   sweetcorn   bean   tomato   raspberry bush   cabbage

Show any working on the back of this sheet.

A 1 How tall is the sunflower plant?

2 How many plants are taller than the bean plant?

3 The height of the raspberry bush is 3 and the height of the tomato plant is 5. How much taller is the tomato plant than the raspberry bush?

B 1 The total height of the tomato plant and the bean plant together is the same as the height of another plant. Which other plant is it?

2 How tall are the sunflower and the sweetcorn plant altogether?

3 How much smaller is the sunflower than the apple tree?

C 1 What is the difference in height between the apple tree and the bean plant?

2 Which plant is half the height of the apple tree?

3 The total height of the sweetcorn plant and the bean plant together is the same as the height of the sunflower plant added to another plant. Which other plant is it?

Skateboarders down a ramp

Chuck

Ella

Ahmed

Delroy

Biku

> Show any working on the back of this sheet.

A 1 Counting from the bottom, which step is Ahmed standing on?

2 Ahmed skates 3 metres. Chuck skates 2 metres. How far do they skate altogether?

3 Ella skates 5 metres and Ahmed skates 3 metres. How many more metres does Ella skate than Ahmed?

B 1 Ella skates 5 metres. Biku skates 3 metres more than Ella. How far does Biku skate?

2 Ella skates 5 metres. Delroy skates 10 metres. How many more metres does Delroy skate than Ella?

3 Ahmed skates 3 metres. Then he starts from a higher step and skates 12 metres. How far does he skate altogether?

C 1 On his first turn, Chuck skates 2 metres. On his second turn he skates 11 metres. How many more metres does he skate on his second time?

2 Ella skates 5 metres. Then she skates 13 metres. What is the difference in metres between her two turns?

3 On Ahmed's second turn he skates 12 metres. On Delroy's second turn, he skates 14 metres. How far do they go altogether?

Anita walks to school

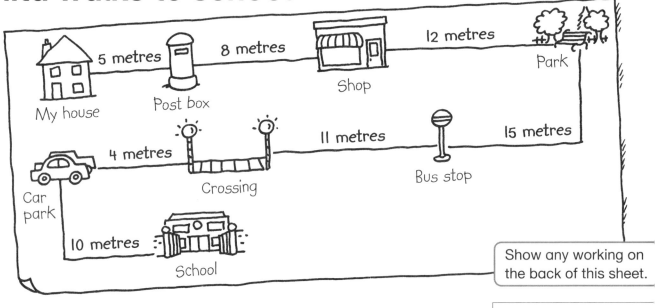

Show any working on the back of this sheet.

A 1 What is between the post box and the park?

2 How many metres does Anita walk from the post box to the shop?

3 Anita goes to post a letter. How far does Anita walk from her house to the post box and back again?

B 1 How far does Anita walk from the crossing to the school?

2 Anita's walk from the park to the bus stop is longer than her walk from the bus stop to the crossing. How much longer?

3 Anita's walk from the crossing to the car park is shorter than her walk from the park to the bus stop. How much shorter?

C 1 How many metres is it altogether from Anita's house to the post box and then on to the shop?

2 How long is Anita's journey from the shop to the bus stop?

3 Roughly how far does Anita walk from her house to school – 30 metres, 60 metres or 90 metres?

Activity 21

Problems involving measures
Geography: 2. How can we make our local area safer?

Name _____

Date _____

Parking in Busy Street

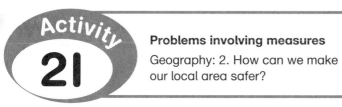

> Show any working on the back of this sheet.

A 1 The butcher parks for 3 hours in the morning and 2 hours in the afternoon. How many hours does he park in the day?

2 The black car parks from 1 o'clock to 3 o'clock. How many hours is this?

3 The butcher parks for 3 hours and the baker parks for 6 hours. How many more hours does the baker park than the butcher?

B 1 The small white car parks for 8 hours on Monday and 8 hours on Tuesday. How many hours does it park altogether on the two days?

2 The Safe Removals van parks for 13 hours on Monday and 6 hours on Tuesday. How many hours does it park altogether on the two days?

3 One day the motor cycle parks for 18 hours and the sports car parks for 5 hours. How much longer does the motor cycle park than the sports car?

C 1 The white car arrives at 9 o'clock in the morning and parks for 8 hours. What time does it leave?

2 The motor cycle parks for 18 hours on Monday and 9 hours on Tuesday. How many hours does it park in the 2 days?

3 The Safe Removals van parks for 13 hours on Monday and 6 hours on Tuesday. How much longer does it park on Monday than Tuesday?

Maths Facts (Y1) © HarperCollinsPublishers Ltd 2003

Barnaby's day in Paris

In the art gallery

On a boat ride

Me at the Eiffel Tower

On the train

> Show any working on the back of this sheet.

A

1 Barnaby left home at 6 o'clock in the morning. It took him I hour to walk to the railway station. What time did he arrive at the station?

2 Barnaby drank I cup of coffee on the train to Paris, 2 cups in Paris and 2 cups on the train home. How many cups is this?

3 In Paris Barnaby went to a café. He ordered 5 cakes but only ate 4 of them. How many cakes were left?

B

1 Barnaby's boat ride started at half past II. The ride lasted 2 hours. At what time did the ride end?

2 The line of people waiting to go up the Eiffel Tower was I7 metres long. After half an hour it was II metres long. How much shorter was it then?

3 Before Barnaby went to Paris he weighed I2 on his scales. When he came back he weighed I6. How much more did he weigh when he came back from Paris?

C

1 Barnaby took an hour and a half to walk to the art gallery. He started at half past 4. What time did he arrive there?

2 Barnaby's train arrived in Paris at half past I0. He spent I0 hours in Paris. The train journey home took 3 hours. He then took I hour to walk home from the station. What time did he get home?

3 The painting Barnaby wanted to see was 24 metres from the door of the art gallery. There were so many people that he could only get 6 metres into the gallery. How far was he from the painting?

A Victorian sitting room

Show any working on the back of this sheet.

A 1 How many pictures and chairs are there?

2 The rug is 2 metres long and the room is 5 metres long. How much longer is the room than the rug?

3 It is 5 o'clock. Jenny goes to bed in 2 hours' time. What time does Jenny go to bed?

B 1 It is 5 o'clock. The family had lunch 5 hours ago. What time did they have lunch?

2 Tom builds a tower of 12 blocks and a tower of 18 blocks. How much taller is one tower than the other?

3 A candle burns for 4 hours. How long would two candles last for?

C 1 Yesterday Mum did 8 rows of knitting. Today she does another 5 rows. How many rows is that altogether?

2 It is 5 o'clock. Mum and Dad go to bed at half past 10. How long is it until they go to bed?

3 After an oil lamp is filled up with oil, it burns for 6 hours. How many hours has it burnt if it is half full?

Activity

24

Problems involving measures
History: 2. What were homes like
a long time ago?

Name _____

Date _____

A Victorian kitchen

Show any working on
the back of this sheet.

A 1 How many blocks of salt weigh the same as 1 cone of sugar?

    2 How many blocks of salt weigh the same as 1 sack of flour?

    3 A sack of flour lasts 10 weeks. How many weeks will
half a sack last?

B 1 It takes 4 pushes of the pump handle to fill the jug. How
many pushes does it take to fill the jug twice?

    2 It takes 4 pushes of the pump handle to fill the jug and
12 pushes to fill the bucket. How many pushes does it take
to fill both the jug and the bucket?

    3 It is 10 o'clock. Lunch is at half past 12. How long
is it until lunch?

C 1 It takes 12 pushes of the pump handle to fill the bucket.
How many pushes does it take to fill 2 buckets?

    2 How many blocks of salt weigh the same as a cone of sugar
and a sack of flour together?

    3 It takes 12 pushes of the pump handle to fill the bucket and
4 pushes to fill the jug. How many more pushes does it take
to fill the bucket than the jug?

Making a cake

Glass

China

Pans

Show any working on the back of this sheet.

A 1 There is a clock in the kitchen. What time is it?

2 There are 3 tea towels and 2 hand towels in one of the drawers. How many towels altogether are in the drawer?

3 In the pan cupboard there are 4 cake tins. If the children use 1 of them, how many cake tins are left in the cupboard?

B 1 The kitchen is 7 metres long and the table is 2 metres long. How much longer is the kitchen than the table?

2 The children use a measuring cup. To make the cake they use 3 cupfuls of flour, 3 cupfuls of sugar, 1 cupful of butter and 1 cupful of milk. How many cupfuls do they use altogether?

3 In the cupboard there are 10 large glasses and 7 small glasses. How many glasses are there altogether in the cupboard?

C 1 In the drawer there are 12 knives and the same number of forks. How many knives and forks are there altogether?

2 The children finish mixing the cake at half past 3. The cake takes 1 hour to cook and half an hour to cool before they can eat it. At what time can they eat it?

3 There are 12 small plates in the china cupboard. The children use 5 of them. How many small plates are left?

Fireworks

> Show any working on the back of this sheet.

A 1 How many fireworks are there between Twinkler and Stars?

2 How many fireworks are taller than Petals?

3 There are 7 fireworks standing in a row. 4 of them have already been lit. How many more are there to light?

B 1 The fireworks start at half past 7 and last for half an hour. At what time do they finish?

2 Everyone pays 10p to watch the fireworks. How much do 9 people pay altogether?

3 In the box there are 12 Twinklers and 6 Stars. How many Twinklers and Stars are there altogether in the box?

C 1 Petals travels 12 metres into the air before exploding. Diamond travels 17 metres before exploding. How many more metres does Diamond travel?

2 Lee and his dad leave home at half past 6. The trip to the fireworks show takes them 1 hour. The show lasts half an hour and the trip home takes another hour. At what time do they get home?

3 In the show 8 Space Rockets and 17 Bombers are let off. How many Space Rockets and Bombers are let off altogether?

Musical instruments

> Show any working on the back of this sheet.

A **1** How many children are there in the band?

2 There are 8 children listening to the band. How many children altogether are listening to the band and playing in it?

3 There are 4 girls in the band. How many more girls are there than boys?

B **1** The music trolley holds 8 tambourines. The band is using 2 of them. How many tambourines are left on the music trolley?

2 It is now half past 10. The band is going to perform at the school assembly in half an hour's time. What time is assembly?

3 The teacher bought each band member a ribbon to wear. Each ribbon cost 10p. How much did the teacher spend?

C **1** On Monday, the band practised for half an hour. On Tuesday and Wednesday they practised for an hour each day. How long has the band practised for?

2 For a music contest the band needs 15 children altogether. How many more children need to join the band?

3 For the music contest, 15 children from the class will be playing in the band and 15 children won't be playing. How many children are in the class?

Activity 28

Problems involving 'real-life' and measures

Geography: 1. Around our school – the local area

Name _____

Date _____

A map of Berry School

> Show any working on the back of this sheet.

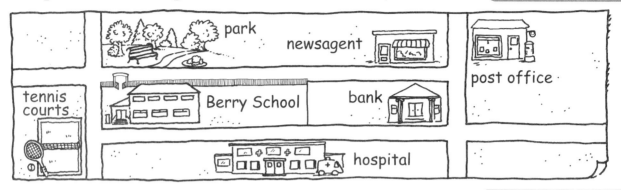

(A) 1 What is opposite the school?

2 How many places are marked on the map?

3 If 4 people play on one tennis court and 2 play on another, how many people are playing tennis?

(B) 1 The tennis courts are used for 2 hours on Monday, 4 hours on Tuesday and 3 hours on Wednesday. How many hours is this altogether?

2 Jo turns left out of the school gate and walks to the end of the street. She then turns left and walks down the street. What place does Jo pass?

3 Harry leaves the school gate and walks 5 metres across the road. He turns right and walks 20 metres to the newsagent. How far does he walk?

(C) 1 It takes Simon half an hour to walk to school. If school starts at 9 o'clock what time does he need to leave home?

2 It is 27 metres from the park to the post office and 20 metres from the park to the newsagent. How many metres is it from the post office to the newsagent?

3 It is 8 metres from the hospital to the bank. It is 15 metres from the bank to the post office. How far is it from the hospital to the post office?

Maths Facts (Y1) © HarperCollins*Publishers* Ltd 2003

Safe Street and Busy Street

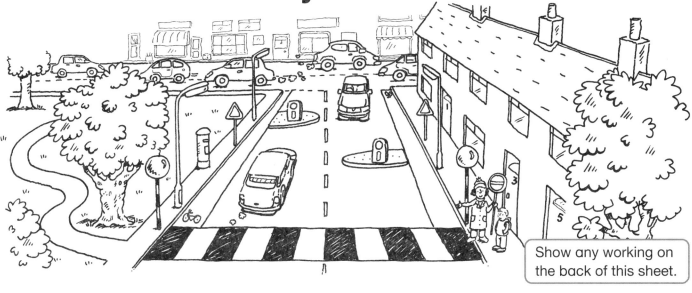

Show any working on the back of this sheet.

A
1. There are 2 cars in Safe Street and 5 cars in Busy Street. How many more cars are there in Busy Street?

2. Are the house numbers you can see in Safe Street odd or even?

3. 2 cars are driving along Safe Street. An hour later 3 cars drive along it. How many cars is that altogether?

B
1. 5 boys and 4 girls live in Safe Street. How many children is this altogether?

2. 10 cats and 7 dogs live in Safe Street. How many more cats than dogs live in Safe Street?

3. Tom walks to school along Safe Street. He spends 10p each afternoon on sweets. How much does he spend in 5 days?

C
1. Add together the odd numbers you can see on the houses in Safe Street.

2. In the morning the lollipop lady helps 20 children cross the street. In the afternoon she helps 14 children. How many children is that altogether?

3. The lollipop lady works from 8 o'clock to 9 o'clock and from 3 o'clock to half past 4. How many hours does she work each day?

Barnaby at the airport

Flight
BY 63

Show any working on the back of this sheet.

A 1 How many bags can you see in the picture?

2 Barnaby can only take 1 bag with him onto the plane. How many bags must he leave at the check-in desk?

3 Barnaby can see 3 planes outside. While he is waiting 2 more planes land. How many planes is that altogether?

B 1 Barnaby's flight is at 4 o'clock. He had to be at the airport 2 hours before his flight. What time did Barnaby have to be at the airport?

2 Barnaby puts 2 bags on the scales. One bag weighs 5 and the other bag weighs 4. How much do they weigh together?

3 When Barnaby went to the check-in desk there were 20 people in front of him. Now there are only 2. How many people have already checked in?

C 1 After checking in, Barnaby buys a comic for 14p and an apple for 13p. How much does he spend altogether?

2 Barnaby got to the airport at half past 1. He left home at 9 o'clock this morning. How long did it take him to get to the airport?

3 Barnaby watches the planes taking off and landing. At first there are 12 planes on the ground. 6 more planes land and 4 planes take off. How many planes are there now on the ground?

Activity
31
Problems involving 'real-life',
money and measures
History: 1. How are our toys
different from those in the past?

Name _____

Date _____

The toy museum

Toys in 1900

Toys in 2000

Show any working on
the back of this sheet.

A 1 How many toys are there altogether?

2 1 of the old toys is a wind-up toy. How many do not wind up?

3 3 of the new toys use batteries. How many of the new toys
do not use batteries?

B 1 When the lead soldiers were new, there were 10 in the box.
Now there are only 4. How many are missing?

2 The museum shop sells sharpeners for 6p and pencils for 5p.
How much do a sharpener and a pencil cost altogether?

3 The museum is open from 9 o'clock to 12 o'clock
and from 1 o'clock to 4 o'clock each day. How
many hours is the museum open for each day?

C 1 Some children visit the museum. 14 go to the Toys in 2000
table and 11 go to the Toys in 1900. How many children
are in the group?

2 In 1900 the rattle cost 9p and the toy theatre cost 7p.
How much did they cost altogether?

3 The batteries in the pocket game last 10 hours and the batteries
in the learning centre last 18 hours. How much
longer do the batteries in the learning centre last?

Beth's family photos

Grandpa in Brighton aged 7

Mum and Auntie Sue in Cornwall

Me last year in Spain

> Show any working on the back of this sheet.

A 1 How many people are there altogether in Mum's photo?

2 When Grandpa was little, ice creams cost 2p. How much did it cost for Grandpa and his dad to have an ice cream each?

3 Auntie Sue is one year younger than Mum. Mum was 8 years old in her photo. How old was Auntie Sue?

B 1 When Grandpa was little, ice creams cost 2p. When Mum was little, ice creams cost 5p more. How much did they cost when Mum was little?

2 Beth went to Spain for 2 weeks. How many days did she go for?

3 There are 16 people in Beth's photo. How many more people are there in Beth's photo than in Mum's?

C 1 When Mum was little it took 14 hours to drive to Cornwall. It took Beth 4 hours to fly to Spain. How much longer did Mum's journey take?

2 Beth stayed on the 17th floor in her hotel in Spain. The roof pool was on the 20th floor. How many floors was it above her?

3 Before her holiday Beth could only swim 14 metres. After her holiday she could swim 8 metres further. How far could she swim after her holiday?

Name _____

Date _____

Humans and animals

Number of legs	
human	2
rabbit	4
dog	4
bird	2
goldfish	0
spider	8

Has ears I can see?	
human	✓
rabbit	✓
dog	✓
bird	✗
goldfish	✗
spider	✗

Has a tail?	
human	✗
rabbit	✓
dog	✓
bird	✓
goldfish	✓
spider	✗

Can swim?	
human	✓
rabbit	✗
dog	✓
bird	✗
goldfish	✓
spider	✗

> Show any working on the back of this sheet.

A 1 How many legs does a bird have?

2 Can dogs swim?

3 How many animals have a tail?

B 1 Which 3 animals do not have ears?

2 Which animal has two legs and no ears?

3 How many animals have ears and more than 2 legs?

C 1 Which animal has 4 legs but cannot swim?

2 Which animal has 4 legs, ears, a tail and can swim?

3 From the tables write down what you know about a spider.

Name _____

Date _____

How are our bodies different?

Eye colour	
James	blue
Max	brown
Sita	hazel
Leroy	brown
Amanda	blue

Hair colour	
James	blond
Max	black
Sita	brown
Leroy	black
Amanda	black

Shoe size	
James	8
Max	10
Sita	8
Leroy	10
Amanda	6

Show any working on the back of this sheet.

A 1 3 boys and 2 girls looked at their hair colour, their eye colour, and the sizes of their shoes. How many children is that altogether?

2 What colour are Sita's eyes?

3 How many children have black hair?

B 1 Who wears size 6 shoes?

2 More children have blue eyes than hazel eyes. How many more children?

3 Who has blue eyes, blond hair and wears size 8 shoes?

C 1 How many children wear shoes larger than Sita?

2 Michael has brown eyes. If you added Michael's name to the table of eye colours, how many children would have brown eyes?

3 Which two children have the same colour eyes, the same colour hair and wear shoes of the same size?

Name _____

Date _____

Growing a sunflower

Week	1	2	3	4	5	6	7	8	9	10
Number of cubes high	2	4	7	10	13	17	20	22	25	25

Week

> Show any working on the back of this sheet.

Ⓐ 1 How many cubes high was the sunflower in week 6?

2 When was the sunflower 7 cubes high?

3 How many cubes high was the sunflower after 10 weeks?

Ⓑ 1 By how many cubes did the sunflower grow between weeks 6 and 7?

2 In week 4 the sunflower was 10 cubes high. In week 7 it was 20 cubes high. What is this difference in height?

3 Between weeks 1 and 2 the sunflower grew by 2 cubes. Between which other 2 weeks did the sunflower also grow by 2 cubes?

Ⓒ 1 By how many cubes did the sunflower grow between weeks 5 and 8?

2 Between which two weeks did the sunflower grow the most?

3 What happened to the sunflower between weeks 9 and 10?

Can Billy hear it?

Billy in the classroom		Billy in the hall	
Mr Smith talking	✓	Mr Smith talking	✗
The school bell	✓	The school bell	✓
An aeroplane in the sky	✓	An aeroplane in the sky	✓
The school choir	✓	The school choir	✓
Billy at the school gate		Billy at home	
Mr Smith talking	✗	Mr Smith talking	✗
The school bell	✓	The school bell	✗
An aeroplane in the sky	✓	An aeroplane in the sky	✓
The school choir	✗	The school choir	✗

Show any working on the back of this sheet.

Ⓐ 1 When Billy is in the hall, can he hear Mr Smith talking?

2 What can Billy hear at home?

3 Where can Billy not hear the school bell?

Ⓑ 1 Where can Billy hear the school choir?

2 What can Billy not hear in the hall, at the school gate or at home?

3 What can Billy hear at the school gate but not at home?

Ⓒ 1 What can Billy hear in the classroom and in the hall, but not at the school gate or at home?

2 What sound can Billy hear everywhere?

3 Put the sounds in order, starting with the loudest.

Activity **37** | **Organising and using data**
Geography: 1. Around our school – the local area | Name _____
Date _____

Around Berry School

Show any working on the back of this sheet.

A **1** How many tennis courts are there near Berry School?

  2 What are most of the buildings around Berry School?

  3 How many parks and tennis courts are there around Berry School?

B **1** There are more shops than parks near Berry School. How many more?

  2 How many more houses are there than shops around Berry School?

  3 There is only one school in the area. What else is there only one of?

C **1** A builder wants to build 6 new houses on one of the parks. How many houses will there be altogether then?

  2 How many more houses are there than tennis courts and parks together around Berry School?

  3 Write a sentence about the number of parks and shops around Berry School.

How children in 1C come to school

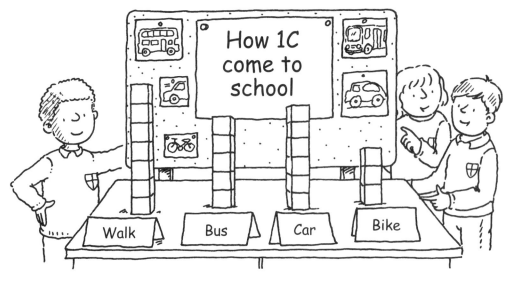

How 1C come to school

Walk   Bus   Car   Bike

Show any working on the back of this sheet.

A 1 How many different ways do the children in IC come to school?

2 How many children walk to school?

3 5 children come to school the same way. Which way is this?

B 1 Do 4 children ride a bike to school?

2 More children come to school by car than by bike. How many more?

3 Put in order the different ways the children come to school, starting with the smallest number.

C 1 Altogether, how many children walk to school or ride a bike?

2 How many children are there altogether in IC?

3 How many children come to school on wheels?

Activity 39

Organising and using data
Geography: 2. How can we make our local area safer?

Name _____

Date _____

Traffic in Safe Street and Busy Street

Safe Street	
In the morning	
bicycles	4
cars	8
motorbikes	6
vans	2
In the afternoon	
bicycles	5
cars	12
motorbikes	4
vans	1

Busy Street	
In the morning	
bicycles	3
cars	29
motorbikes	14
vans	16
In the afternoon	
bicycles	3
cars	26
motorbikes	18
vans	11

Show any working on the back of this sheet.

Ⓐ 1 How many cars travelled along Safe Street in the morning?

2 How many motorbikes travelled along Busy Street in the morning?

3 How many cars and vans altogether travelled along Safe Street in the morning?

Ⓑ 1 More cars than vans travelled along Safe Street in the morning. How many more?

2 Were there more bicycles, cars, motorbikes or vans travelling along Safe Street in the morning?

3 Did more motorbikes travel along Safe Street or Busy Street during the whole day?

Ⓒ 1 How many vans travelled along Busy Street during the whole day?

2 More motorbikes than vans travelled along Busy Street in the afternoon. How many more?

3 During the whole day more bicycles travelled along Safe Street than along Busy Street. How many more?

Activity
40

Organising and using data
History: 1. How are our toys
different from those in the past?

Name _____

Date _____

Show any working on
the back of this sheet.

A 1 How many toys are there on the grandparents' table?

2 How many toys altogether have been mended?

3 How many toys altogether have been sorted?

B 1 Which 2 toys on the grandparents' table are wooden?

2 How many toys altogether use batteries?

3 How many toys are broken and have not been mended?

C 1 The toys are sorted onto 2 tables – toys with wheels and
toys without wheels. How many toys are there on the table
for toys with wheels?

2 The toys are sorted onto 3 tables – not broken, broken and
mended, broken and not mended. How many toys are there
on the table for toys that are not broken?

3 How else could you sort these toys?

Answers

Activity 1
Our bodies

A 1 20
    2 6
    3 10 years old

B 1 3 years
    2 4
    3 40

C 1 4
    2 5
    3 16

Activity 2
Young and old

A 1 3 years old
    2 3 years
    3 7 years old

B 1 5 years old
    2 3 years
    3 11 years old

C 1 40 years old
    2 36 years old
    3 4 years

Activity 3
Different lights

A 1 9
    2 7
    3 5

B 1 2
    2 17
    3 3

C 1 2
    2 5
    3 24

Activity 4
Playing safe in the sun

A 1 13
    2 22
    3 3

B 1 4
    2 4
    3 11

C 1 9
    2 13
    3 12

Activity 5
The wind

A 1 6
    2 6
    3 5

B 1 12
    2 6
    3 3

C 1 3
    2 9
    3 12

Activity 6
An Edwardian country house

A 1 25
    2 10
    3 6

B 1 6
    2 20
    3 9

C 1 14
    2 5
    3 17

Activity 7
An Edwardian kitchen

A 1 11
    2 7
    3 2

B 1 5
    2 4
    3 5

C 1 30
    2 4
    3 9

Activity 8
On the beach in 1900

A 1 4
    2 9
    3 3

B 1 2
    2 2
    3 4

C 1 8
    2 8
    3 16

Activity 9
Food and drink

A 1 2
    2 2p
    3 4p

B 1 3p
    2 5p, 2p, 1p
    3 14p

C 1 22p
    2 5p
    3 25p

Answers

Activity 10
Food we eat from seeds

A 1 8p
  2 3p
  3 10p

B 1 lettuce seeds
  2 16p
  3 13p

C 1 5p, 2p, 2p
  2 0p
  3 9p

Activity 11
The hardware shop

A 1 8
  2 2p
  3 3p, 5p, 11p, 13p, 14p, 15p, 16p, 18p

B 1 a plug
  2 2p
  3 16p

C 1 10p, 5p, 1p
  2 7p
  3 a watering can

Activity 12
The post office

A 1 6
  2 3p
  3 6p

B 1 20p
  2 8p
  3 16p

C 1 5p
  2 50p
  3 10p and 12p

Activity 13
The community sports centre

A 1 bowling
  2 1p
  3 5p, 6p, 9p, 12p, 14p, 16p

B 1 12p
  2 19p
  3 6p

C 1 no
  2 played squash
  3 20p

Activity 14
Barnaby's shopping list

A 1 9
  2 5
  3 2p, 4p, 6p, 7p, 9p, 10p, 11p, 12p, 20p

B 1 29p
  2 18p
  3 1p

C 1 4p
  2 20p coin
  3 80p

Activity 15
Old toys for sale

A 1 12
  2 skittles and blocks
  3 4p

B 1 3
  2 22p
  3 yes

C 1 10p, 2p, 1p
  2 9p
  3 18p

Activity 16
Annie's seaside holiday

A 1 1p
  2 6p
  3 3p, 4p, 5p, 9p, 12p, 14p

B 1 10p
  2 no
  3 20p

C 1 10p, 2p, 2p
  2 28p
  3 23p

Activity 17
Measuring heights

A 1 6
  2 8 blocks
  3 Leo, Ali, Gita, Jini, Sam, Mrs James

B 1 6 blocks
  2 15 blocks
  3 16 blocks

C 1 9 blocks
  2 3 blocks
  3 28 blocks

Activity 18
Plants that feed us

A 1 12
  2 3
  3 2

B 1 sunflower
  2 20
  3 4

C 1 9
  2 sweetcorn
  3 raspberry bush

Activity 19
Skateboarders down a ramp

A 1 4th
   2 5 metres
   3 2 metres

B 1 8 metres
   2 5 metres
   3 15 metres

C 1 9 metres
   2 8 metres
   3 26 metres

Activity 20
Anita walks to school

A 1 shop
   2 8 metres
   3 10 metres

B 1 14 metres
   2 4 metres
   3 11 metres

C 1 13 metres
   2 27 metres
   3 60 metres

Activity 21
Parking in Busy Street

A 1 5 hours
   2 2 hours
   3 3 hours

B 1 16 hours
   2 19 hours
   3 13 hours

C 1 5 o'clock
   2 27 hours
   3 7 hours

Activity 22
Barnaby's day in Paris

A 1 7 o'clock
   2 5
   3 1

B 1 half past 1
   2 6 metres
   3 4

C 1 6 o'clock
   2 half past 12
   3 18 metres

Activity 23
A Victorian sitting room

A 1 4
   2 3 metres
   3 7 o'clock

B 1 12 o'clock
   2 6
   3 8 hours

C 1 13
   2 $5\frac{1}{2}$ hours
   3 3 hours

Activity 24
A Victorian kitchen

A 1 2
   2 5
   3 5 weeks

B 1 8
   2 16
   3 $2\frac{1}{2}$ hours

C 1 24
   2 7
   3 8

Activity 25
Making a cake

A 1 3 o'clock
   2 5
   3 3

B 1 5 metres
   2 8
   3 17

C 1 24
   2 5 o'clock
   3 7

Activity 26
Fireworks

A 1 3
   2 4
   3 3

B 1 8 o'clock
   2 90p
   3 18

C 1 5 metres
   2 9 o'clock
   3 25

Activity 27
Musical instruments

A 1 7
   2 15
   3 1

B 1 6
   2 11 o'clock
   3 70p

C 1 $2\frac{1}{2}$ hours
   2 8
   3 30

Activity 28
A map of Berry School

A 1 a park
   2 7
   3 6

B 1 9 hours
   2 tennis courts
   3 25 metres

C 1 half past 8
   2 7 metres
   3 23 metres

Activity 29
Safe Street and Busy Street

A 1 3
   2 odd
   3 5

B 1 9
   2 3
   3 50p

C 1 9
   2 34
   3 $2\frac{1}{2}$ hours

Activity 30
Barnaby at the airport

A 1 12
   2 2
   3 5

B 1 2 o'clock
   2 9
   3 18

C 1 27p
   2 $4\frac{1}{2}$ hours
   3 14

Activity 31
The toy museum

A 1 10
   2 4
   3 2

B 1 6
   2 11p
   3 6 hours

C 1 25
   2 16p
   3 8 hours

Activity 32
Beth's family photos

A 1 6
   2 4p
   3 7 years old

B 1 7p
   2 14 days
   3 10

C 1 10 hours
   2 3
   3 22 metres

Activity 33
Humans and animals

A 1 2
   2 yes
   3 4

B 1 bird, goldfish, spider
   2 bird
   3 2

C 1 rabbit
   2 dog
   3 e.g. Has 8 legs, no
      ears, no tail and
      cannot swim.

Activity 34
How are our bodies different?

A 1 5
   2 hazel
   3 3

B 1 Amanda
   2 1
   3 James

C 1 2
   2 3
   3 Max and Leroy

Activity 35
Growing a sunflower

A 1 17
   2 week 3
   3 25

B 1 3
   2 10 cubes
   3 weeks 7 and 8

C 1 9
   2 weeks 5 and 6
   3 e.g. It did not grow
      any higher.

Activity 36
Can Billy hear it?

A 1 no
   2 an aeroplane in the sky
   3 at home

B 1 in the classroom and
      in the hall
   2 Mr Smith talking
   3 the school bell

C 1 the school choir
2 an aeroplane in the sky
3 an aeroplane in the sky, the school bell, the school choir, Mr Smith talking

Activity 37
Around Berry School

A 1 3
2 houses
3 5

B 1 4
2 3
3 hospital

C 1 15
2 4
3 e.g. There are 6 shops and 2 parks around Berry School.
There are more shops than parks around Berry School.
There are fewer parks than shops around Berry School.

Activity 38
How children in 1C come to school

A 1 4
2 7
3 bus

B 1 no
2 3
3 bike, bus, car, walk or 3, 5, 6, 7

C 1 10
2 21
3 14

Activity 39
Traffic in Safe Street and Busy Street

A 1 8
2 14
3 10

B 1 6
2 cars
3 Busy Street

C 1 27
2 7
3 3

Activity 40
Sorting toys

A 1 6
2 2
3 16

B 1 tennis racket and jigsaw puzzle
2 3
3 2

C 1 8
2 12
3 e.g. Whether it is a sporting toy or not a sporting toy.
The material used to make the toy.
Toys you can wear.